CLEOPATRA
THE QUEEN OF KINGS

DATE DUE

Julius Caesar

Cleopatra is summoned to Tarsus by Antony.

Cleopatra rewards a loyal subject with a gold necklace.

A *millefiori* (thousands of flowers) glass drinking cup

Cleopatra's younger brother seizes power.

A coin decorated with a cornucopia (horn of plenty)

Craftsmen work on Cleopatra's mausoleum

CLEOPATRA
THE QUEEN OF KINGS

Written by
FIONA MACDONALD

Illustrated by
CHRIS MOLAN

LONDON, NEW YORK, MUNICH,
MELBOURNE, and DELHI

Project Editor Sue Barraclough
Art Editor Catherine Goldsmith
Senior Editor Marie Greenwood
Senior Art Editor Carole Oliver
Publishing Manager Jayne Parsons
Managing Art Editor Jacquie Gulliver
DTP Designer Nomazwe Madonko
Picture Researcher Franziska Marking
Jacket Designer Dean Price
Production Kate Oliver
Consultant Dr. Sally-Ann Ashton
Special photography Max Alexander, Alistair Duncan,
Christi Graham and Nick Nichols, Peter Hayam, John Heseltine,
Dave King, Stephen Oliver, Lawrence Pardes, Tony Souter

Additional illustrations by John James

This edition published in the United States in 2006
by DK Publishing, Inc.
375 Hudson Street,
New York, New York 10014

06 07 08 09 10 10 9 8 7 6 5 4 3 2 1

DK books are available at special discounts for bulk purchases for sales
promotions, premiums, fund-raising, or educational use. For details, contact:
DK Publishing Special Markets
375 Hudson Street
New York, NY 10014
SpecialSales@dk.com

A catalog record for this book is available from the Library of Congress.

ISBN-13 978-0-789477-61-3 ISBN-10 0-7894-7761-0 (Hardcover)
ISBN-13 978-0-756619-64-0 ISBN-10 0-7566-1964-5 (Paperback)

Color reproduction by Colourscan, Singapore
Printed in China by Toppan Printing Co. (Shenzhen) Ltd.

Discover more at
www.dk.com

Contents

Cleopatra's Egypt

FOR OVER 3,000 YEARS, EGYPT WAS HOME TO A RICH and splendid civilization. But by 69 BC, when Cleopatra VII was born, Egypt's power was failing. The country was ruled by a dynasty (family) of pharaohs, all called Ptolemy, who had arrived from Macedonia in 323 BC. Egypt was also in danger of being taken over by its great rival, Rome. The first Ptolemies had ruled well, but their descendants, including Cleopatra's father, were weak and even foolish. Cleopatra faced an uncertain future. But she was to become a daring and courageous queen, and one of the most famous women who has ever lived.

Harold Oakley's watercolor of the Pharos is based on a reconstruction, made in the late 19th century.

Alexandria, Cleopatra's home, was a bustling port on the Mediterranean Sea. The early Ptolemies encouraged science, art, and trade and introduced many new ideas and inventions to Egypt.

The Pharos tower was the world's first lighthouse. Built around 280 BC, it was destroyed by an earthquake in the 14th century. Today it is remembered as one of the Seven Wonders of the Ancient World.

Harold Oakley

FAMILY AT WAR

FROM AN EARLY AGE, CLEOPATRA knew that her family was at war – with the people it ruled, and with itself. The people suffered under the cruelty of Cleopatra's father – Ptolemy XII – and they resented his alliance with Rome. In 58 BC, the citizens of Alexandria rioted and chased Ptolemy out of Egypt. Ptolemy fled to Rome, and Cleopatra's older sister, Berenice, became queen. In 55 BC, Ptolemy returned to Egypt. Helped by Roman general Pompey, he snatched back power from Berenice and ruled as pharoah (king) once more. Ptolemy then gave orders for Berenice to be executed.

Pompey the Great
Pompey (106–48 BC) was one of the most brilliant generals of his time. By helping Ptolemy XII he hoped to increase Roman power in Egypt.

RIVALS FOR POWER
All Ptolemy XII's children hoped to rule, and this made them rivals. Cleopatra's older sister, Berenice IV, ruled from 58–55 BC. Her sister, Cleopatra Tryphaena, died mysteriously around this time – the rumor was that Berenice had murdered her.

CLEOPATRA VII
At 14 Cleopatra had seen her father flee for his life and family members killed. She must have wondered how long she would survive.

PTOLEMY XII
Ptolemy XII was pharoah of Egypt during the years 80–58 BC and 55–51 BC. Ptolemy was disliked by his subjects because he collected heavy taxes and sent the money to Rome. Ptolemy hoped that if he made friends with the Roman leaders and paid the Romans enough money, they would not invade his land.

| Ptolemy XIII | Ptolemy XIV | Berenice | Cleopatra Tryphaena | Arsinoe |

CLEOPATRA'S BROTHERS
Cleopatra had two younger brothers, both called Ptolemy according to family custom. They were both to become rulers of Egypt – as Ptolemy XIII and Ptolemy XIV.

CLEOPATRA'S SISTERS
Ptolemy had four daughters. Cleopatra's sisters were called Berenice IV, Cleopatra Tryphaena VI, and Arsinoe IV. By 55 BC Cleopatra had only one sister still alive – the youngest, Arsinoe.

Portrait of Ptolemy XII
The Ptolemies paid to have their portraits carved in ancient Egyptian style, even though they were from Macedonia (northern Greece). They wanted to link themselves with the great pharoahs of Egypt's past. This carving, at the Temple of Horus at Edfu, shows Ptolemy XII conquering his enemies.

Symbols of power

CLEOPATRA'S FAMILY, the Ptolemies, introduced many changes to Egypt. One of the most important was the use of coins for trade. Before the Ptolemies, coins were almost unknown; Egyptian merchants bartered (exchanged) goods instead. Coins also carried a political message. Images on the Ptolemies' coins showed them as rich and powerful.

This beautiful portrait shows a Ptolemaic queen – Berenice II, sister and wife of Ptolemy III.

A cornucopia (horn overflowing with fruit and grain) – symbol of wealth and prosperity.

THE ROMAN EMPIRE
While the Ptolemies faced problems in Egypt, the Roman empire continued to expand. By 55 BC the Roman army had conquered land in northern and southern Europe, in north Africa, and in the Middle East.

The Roman army was a formidable fighting machine. Many thousands of well-trained soldiers marched into battle to win new lands for Rome.

The coast around the Nile Delta was very flat, so the huge lighthouse helped ships find their way into Alexandria harbor.

Alexandria was a flourishing port on the Mediterranean. The rulers of Rome relied on Egypt to supply the people of its empire with grain and other foodstuffs.

Nile Delta

FRANCE

GREECE

● Rome
ITALY

● Actium

SPAIN

MEDITERRANEAN SEA

●Alexandria
EGYPT

Between c. 200–55 BC the Roman empire expanded so rapidly that Rome often had to rely on "puppet" kings to run the countries for them.

THE SUN GOD'S DAUGHTER

CLEOPATRA WAS NOW PTOLEMY XII'S oldest surviving child. When he died she would become queen, as the wife of her younger brother, Ptolemy XIII. This was exciting, but also terrifying. Cleopatra remembered what had happened to her sisters, and feared that enemies might try to kill her too. But Cleopatra was clever. She made friends with powerful courtiers. She prepared herself for government by learning many languages including Egyptian (all the other members of her family only spoke Greek). She also used religion to support her claim to the throne. Cleopatra called herself the sun god's daughter, which was an ancient royal title.

Homes for the gods
Temples were built as homes for the gods. The priests made offerings of food, drink, and incense to the holy statues every day. The more important temples were wealthy, powerful organizations. They owned farms, orchards, libraries, and workshops, and employed many servants.

The sacred bull of Buchis
Egyptians believed that the sacred bulls, in a temple at Buchis, were the sun god Amun-Re in animal form. Soon after she became queen, Cleopatra traveled down the Nile with a newly chosen Buchis bull. To the Egyptian people, the bulls were gods, and by taking part in the ceremony, Cleopatra was showing the people that she respected their gods.

Inner shrine
Only members of the royal family or senior priests and priestesses could enter the dark inner shrine of each temple, where the statue of the god or goddess stood.

MAKING MUSIC
Musicians, singers, and dancers performed holy music while Cleopatra made offerings of food and flowers.

Gods and goddesses

LIKE ALL THE Ptolemies and their queens before her, Cleopatra said prayers and made offerings to many of the gods and goddesses of ancient Egypt. Traditionally, Isis and Hathor protected Egyptian queens from harm.

Amun Re, lord of the sun, was the mightiest god of all.

Isis was goddess of magic and healing.

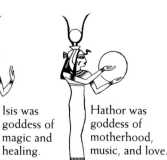

Hathor was goddess of motherhood, music, and love.

" The Queen, the Lady of the Two Lands, the father-loving goddess, rowed the Bull in the barge of Amon to Hermonthis. **"**

Translated from a stele
(stone slab) at Hermonthis
(now called Amant).

POWERFUL FRIENDS

Cleopatra needed the support of priests who belonged to rich, powerful families. All priests received a share of offerings made to the gods, and of the profits from temple lands. Priests spent time away from their temples and many served as senior officials at court. So Cleopatra gave generous gifts to the most important temples, to encourage their priests to help her stay in power.

INSIDE THE
TEMPLE
*To reach the inner
shrine, worshippers
walked in a solemn
procession through the
great hypostyle hall at
the front of the temple,
with its massive carved
and painted columns.*

MAGNIFICENT HEADDRESS
*Like other Ptolemaic queens,
Cleopatra wore a tall headdress
of gold plumes (symbol of the
god Amun), with a sun disk
and a pair of horns (symbols of
the goddesses Hathor and Isis).*

*Sweet-smelling incense was
burned as an offering to the gods.*

11

Teenage Queen

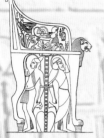

An Egyptian throne – a symbol of royal power.

ANCIENT RECORDS INDICATE THAT CLEOPATRA RULED with her father for a short time. And after his death in 51 BC, 18-year-old Cleopatra was determined to hold on to power. In keeping with the traditions of the time, she married her 12-year-old brother, Ptolemy XIII. (Like all the Ptolemies before her, she did not want to marry outside the royal family because that might weaken its power.) In law, Ptolemy now had the right to rule, but his sister said that he was too young. Cleopatra wanted to rule – alone. However, Cleopatra knew that many nobles and royal officials supported her brother's right to rule. And General Pompey, her dead father's powerful ally, had plans to govern Egypt for Rome. The young Cleopatra knew she would need to use all her charm and intelligence to remain queen.

A carved relief in traditional Egyptian style at the Temple of Hathor at Dendera.

> "If Cleopatra's nose had been shorter, the whole face of the world would have been changed."
>
> Blaise Pascal (French philosopher), commenting on Cleopatra's legendary beauty. From his *Pensées* (Thoughts) c.1670.

ROYAL PORTRAIT
Cleopatra clearly
had a powerful
and fascinating
personality, even
when young. So
throughout history,
she has always been
portrayed as beautiful,
as in this marble head.
However, nobody knows for
sure what she actually looked like.

LIFE IN CLEOPATRA'S EGYPT

CLEOPATRA AND HER FAMILY LIVED IN Alexandria, Egypt's splendid capital city. The city had been founded by Alexander the Great in 331 BC, and it had grown and prospered over 300 years of rule by the Ptolemies. Alexandria was one of the most important ports in the ancient world, and it was home to an exciting multicultural civilization, which blended Greek, Egyptian, and Middle Eastern ideas and beliefs. But to most ordinary Egyptians, Alexandria seemed strange and foreign – just like the Ptolemies themselves. In the first two years of Cleopatra's reign the Nile failed to flood. There were crop failures and famines, and many ordinary people starved. As ruler of Egypt, Cleopatra needed to help the people and win their support – but she also needed to please the sophisticated citizens of Alexandria.

Waterwheel
This beautiful wall painting shows an ox harnessed to a *sakkiyeh* (a wooden waterwheel). As the ox walked round, the wheel turned, lifting water from the Nile to the fields. Oxen still pull waterwheels in Egypt today.

> ❝For by nature the land produces more fruit than do other lands, and still more when watered...❞
>
> Strabo, from
> *Geography*, c. 100 BC

FACT file

- The Nile is the world's longest river. It runs for 4,160 miles (6,690 km) from the highlands of central Africa to the Mediterranean Sea.

- Today, the Nile is dammed at Aswan, but in Cleopatra's time it flooded in June because of rainwater it carried from the highlands. The land beside the river remained underwater until August or September.

- After the floods, the land was covered in thick, fertile mud. It was dry enough to plow by November, the start of the Egyptian farmers' year.

TRAVELING BY BOAT

This wooden model of a boat was found in a tomb. Egyptians would have sailed up and down the Nile to take crops to market, to visit temples, and to trade.

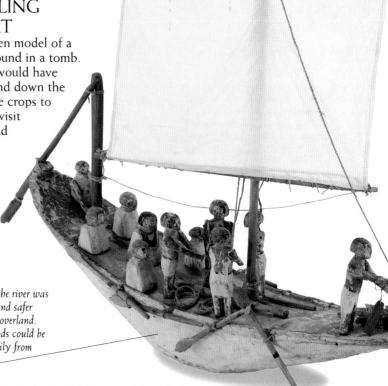

UNDER SAIL
Sailing along the river was much quicker and safer than traveling overland. People and goods could be transported easily from place to place.

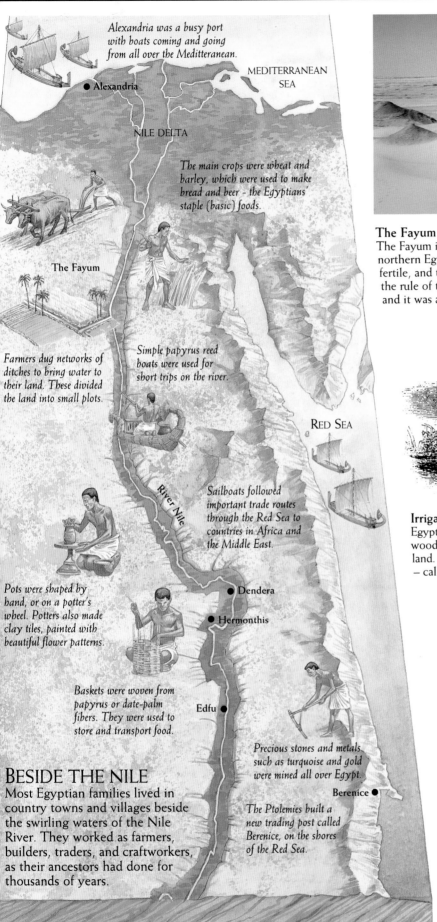

Alexandria was a busy port with boats coming and going from all over the Meditteranean.

● Alexandria

MEDITERRANEAN SEA

NILE DELTA

The main crops were wheat and barley, which were used to make bread and beer - the Egyptians' staple (basic) foods.

The Fayum

Farmers dug networks of ditches to bring water to their land. These divided the land into small plots.

Simple papyrus reed boats were used for short trips on the river.

River Nile

RED SEA

Sailboats followed important trade routes through the Red Sea to countries in Africa and the Middle East.

Pots were shaped by hand, or on a potter's wheel. Potters also made clay tiles, painted with beautiful flower patterns.

● Dendera

● Hermonthis

Baskets were woven from papyrus or date-palm fibers. They were used to store and transport food.

Edfu ●

Precious stones and metals such as turquoise and gold were mined all over Egypt.

Berenice ●

The Ptolemies built a new trading post called Berenice, on the shores of the Red Sea.

BESIDE THE NILE

Most Egyptian families lived in country towns and villages beside the swirling waters of the Nile River. They worked as farmers, builders, traders, and craftworkers, as their ancestors had done for thousands of years.

The Fayum

The Fayum is a large area of low-lying land in the desert of northern Egypt, surrounding a freshwater lake. The soil is fertile, and the lake provides water for growing crops. Under the rule of the Ptolemies many Greek settlers moved there, and it was a busy and prosperous area.

Irrigation – watering the land

Egyptian farmers also used a *shaduf* (a bucket fixed to a long wooden arm) to lift water from the river to irrigate their land. The Ptolemies introduced a machine for lifting water – called an Archimedian Screw – from Greece to Egypt.

More wine!

BEFORE THE RULE of the Ptolemies wine was rare and expensive, and most Egyptians drank beer. The Greeks preferred wine so they brought new wine-making skills to Egypt.

This wall painting shows farm workers harvesting and treading grapes.

INTO EXILE

FOR THE FIRST TWO YEARS OF HER REIGN Cleopatra managed to keep control of Egypt, but she had many enemies. One of the most powerful was Pothinus, her brother Ptolemy's chief adviser. He did not like the way Cleopatra made many important government decisions without consulting him. Also, Ptolemy XIII was nearly 16 years old and was demanding his share of power. In 48 BC, Cleopatra discovered that Ptolemy and Pothinus were plotting to send soldiers to kidnap her and guessed that they planned to kill her. Cleopatra knew that she must leave Egypt. She set sail for Syria. There, Cleopatra hoped to recruit an army, to help her win back her throne from her brother who had now seized the throne.

Ptolemy's advisers
Young Ptolemy XIII relied heavily on advice given by top official Pothinus and leaders of rival groups of nobles at the Egyptian royal court.

Ruling alone
Cleopatra angered Ptolemy XIII and his supporters with displays of her own power, like this bronze coin, struck early in her reign. It carries her portrait and does not show her brother and coruler.

SEEKING SUPPORT
Cleopatra chose to go to Syria because the Ptolemies had once ruled there. The king of Syria was also an enemy of Rome. Like Cleopatra, he feared that his own country would be taken over by the mighty Roman empire.

SISTERS TOGETHER
Cleopatra took her only surviving sister, Arsinoe, into exile with her. This was partly to protect her from Ptolemy and Pothinus, but more importantly to stop Arsinoe from trying to seize power.

DANGEROUS JOURNEY
It was a dangerous journey to Syria. The Mediterranean Sea was often troubled by violent squalls, and shipwrecks were common.

BATTLE FOR POWER

Julius Caesar and Pompey had once been close comrades, but in 48 BC they became rivals for supreme power in Rome. Their clash led to fighting between rival Roman armies, ending with the Battle of Pharsalus at which Julius Caesar was victorious.

Julius Caesar

Pharsalus

SYRIA

Cleopatra traveled back overland to Egypt.

MEDITERRANEAN SEA

Cleopatra's ship

Alexandria

EGYPT

After the Battle of Pharsalus, Pompey sailed directly to Egypt. Caesar was never far behind him.

A TREACHEROUS ACT

While Cleopatra sought help in Syria, her guardian Pompey hurried to Egypt where he hoped that Ptolemy and Cleopatra would offer him money and soldiers. But Ptolemy's supporters murdered Pompey as soon as he landed in Alexandria.

Pompey

KEEPING WATCH
Lookouts kept watch for pirates who raided ships with valuable cargo.

> "It was a delight to hear the sound of her voice. As if her voice were an instrument of many strings, she could pass from one language to another ... and she seldom needed an interpreter."

Plutarch, from his
*Life of Mark
Antony,* c. AD 75

CLEVER AND CHARMING

CAESAR ARRIVED IN EGYPT IN 48 BC, just four days after Pompey was killed. When Caesar landed at Alexandria, Ptolemy XIII's supporters offered him Pompey's head as a gift. Caesar was horrified. However, he had come to Egypt to collect a huge sum of money that he claimed Cleopatra's father had owed him, so he wanted to keep the peace. He ordered Cleopatra and Ptolemy to meet with him to discuss a peace treaty. Cleopatra did not trust her brother, and knew that there was a real danger that she would be killed if she came face to face with any of his advisers. She knew that she needed Caesar's protection. One night Cleopatra had herself smuggled into Caesar's room – she was about to use all her charm and intelligence to win his support.

UNDERCOVER
Some stories say that Cleopatra was hidden in a carpet and some inside a roll of bedding.

Courage and loyalty
A merchant called Apollodorus was persuaded by Cleopatra to risk his life to smuggle her into the heavily-guarded palace.

HIDDEN CHARMS
Caesar was astonished when the carpet was unrolled to reveal Cleopatra herself.

A GIFT FOR CAESAR
Rulers like Cleopatra often sent rich gifts to powerful people. So Caesar would not have been surprised when Cleopatra's servant brought him a beautiful carpet. Cleopatra quickly gained Caesar's support but she still had enemies in Alexandria. Caesar, who had arrived with only a small army of men, was happy to find an ally in such a hostile city.

Caesar's barber

Pothinus sent a message to Achillas outside the city, outlining his plan to murder Caesar.

A servant would have carried the message out of the palace.

PLOT AGAINST CAESAR

When Pothinus, Ptolemy's chief adviser, found out that Cleopatra had won Caesar's support, he plotted against him. Caesar's barber heard Pothinus's plans, and Pothinus was executed. Meanwhile Arsinoe escaped from the city to join forces with Achillas and the army against Caesar.

JULIUS CAESAR
Impressed by Cleopatra's courage and daring, Caesar was soon bewitched by her.

City of learning

Cleopatra used her knowledge and intelligence to stay in power. The Ptolemies helped to make Alexandria into a great center of learning. In Cleopatra's time the library was the greatest in the world.

Hieroglyphs
Demotic
Greek

The Rosetta Stone

Texts of the three languages used in Egypt in Cleopatra's time can be seen on the Rosetta Stone: hieroglyphs (used for royal decrees and religious texts); demotic (a written, simplified form of hieroglyphs); and Greek (Cleopatra's mother tongue). Cleopatra was famous for her knowledge of these languages and many others.

The Rosetta Stone is a slab of basalt rock found near Rosetta in the Nile delta.

PTOLEMY'S FURY

Ptolemy XIII ran out of the palace and threw down his crown in rage when he heard that Cleopatra had reached Caesar. With the royal quarter under siege, Caesar let Ptolemy leave the city to join General Achillas, his sister Arsinoe, and the Egyptian army. Days after the war in Alexandria ended Ptolemy's body was found in the harbor.

ROYAL BEAUTY

CLEOPATRA KNEW THAT LOOKING good was important. An impressive appearance helped her to get her own way – with Caesar, and with the Egyptian people too. She chose what she wore for each occasion with care. It is thought that for official public duties, Cleopatra wore Egyptian costume – a long, pleated linen shift decorated with beads and embroidery. In the privacy of her palace, Cleopatra probably preferred Greek-style robes of soft linen or smooth silk. Whatever the occasion, Cleopatra knew that she must appear impressive, powerful, and in control.

KEEPING CLEAN

All Egyptians liked to feel clean and fresh. Wealthy Egyptians, like Cleopatra, would have had baths, while ordinary people washed in the Nile River.

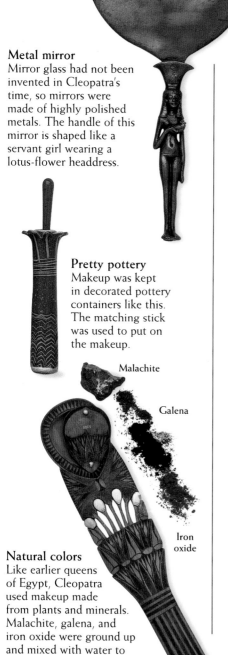

Metal mirror
Mirror glass had not been invented in Cleopatra's time, so mirrors were made of highly polished metals. The handle of this mirror is shaped like a servant girl wearing a lotus-flower headdress.

Pretty pottery
Makeup was kept in decorated pottery containers like this. The matching stick was used to put on the makeup.

Malachite

Galena

Iron oxide

Natural colors
Like earlier queens of Egypt, Cleopatra used makeup made from plants and minerals. Malachite, galena, and iron oxide were ground up and mixed with water to make colorings for lips, eyes, and cheeks.

Fragrances and flowers
The Egyptians valued the sacred lotus flower for its delicate perfume. They also made perfumes with oils made from fragrant woods like cedar, and from cinnamon, honey, myrrh, and henna.

HELPING HANDS
After bathing, Cleopatra's servants wrapped her in soft linen towels, and massaged her skin with fragrant oils.

Sweet-smelling lotus (water lily) flowers were symbols of rebirth and new life after death.

LOOKING LIKE A QUEEN

With her traditional Egyptian gown, Cleopatra wore a heavy wig. She also wore thick makeup, Egyptian style. Her eyelids were colored, her eyes were outlined, and her cheeks were rouged.

Ocher (red earth) or plant and seaweed extracts were painted onto tint lips.

Cleopatra wore soft leather sandals with metal trimmings.

SACRED CREATURES
Cats were sacred. A Roman was stoned to death in Alexandria for accidentally killing a cat.

Images of Cleopatra

WE DO NOT know what Cleopatra looked like – all the portraits that have survived look very different. The features and hairstyle of this Roman head match her coin portraits, but Cleopatra would always have worn a diadem (crown). Egyptian portraits show Cleopatra as a goddess, and were not intended to be lifelike.

Roman head

Traditional Egyptian carving

FINISHING TOUCHES

Cleopatra wore beautiful jewelry, elaborate makeup, and rich perfume. Sometimes, her nails and the palms of her hands were decorated with patterns in henna.

ROYAL SYMBOL
The cobra represented the goddess Wadjet who was believed to protect kings and queens.

" Her beauty was not so striking that it stunned the onlooker, but she made an inescapable impression on people around her ... the intelligence of all that she said and did was bewitching. "

Plutarch, from his
Life of Mark Antony,
c. AD 75

A Powerful Protector

JULIUS CAESAR
Caesar was a brilliant army commander and ambitious ruler of Rome.

FOR THE FIRST TIME IN YEARS, CLEOPATRA felt secure. Her enemy Ptolemy XIII and his advisers were dead, and Caesar promised to protect her and her new husband – her surviving brother, 11-year-old Ptolemy XIV. With Caesar, she sailed down the Nile, to meet her subjects and impress them with her power. Rumors said that Cleopatra was pregnant with Caesar's child. When Caesar returned to Rome, he left 15,000 men to guard her.

The temple walls were decorated with carved reliefs. Huge portraits of Cleopatra and her son Caesarion (Caesar's child) were later carved here.

66 The eldest of Ptolemy's sons being dead, Caesar settled the kingdom upon the youngest, in conjunction with Cleopatra, the elder of the two sisters, who had always continued under his protection and guardianship. 99

Written by one of Julius Caesar's officers, from *The Alexandrian War*, 47 BC

The temple of Hathor, Dendera. Cleopatra may have visited the temple to make offerings to the goddess Hathor on her Nile cruise with Caesar.

TO CAESAR'S ROME

AFTER TAKING CONTROL IN EGYPT, Caesar returned to Rome in 46 BC where he was welcomed as a hero. Cleopatra soon hurried to join him. She claimed that she was negotiating a peace treaty between Egypt and Rome, but she also wanted to make sure of Caesar's protection. Cleopatra brought her son Caesarion and teenage pharoah Ptolemy XIV with her. She did not want her brother or his advisers to try to seize power in Egypt while she was away. Many Romans were shocked by the relationship between Caesar and Cleopatra. They were afraid that Caesar would name Caesarion as his heir – that Cleopatra's son could become ruler of Rome.

Arriving in Rome
This scene, from a Hollywood film called *Cleopatra* made in 1963, shows Cleopatra (played by Elizabeth Taylor) arriving in Rome with her son Caesarion.

TRIUMPH
The victory procession, or "triumph," was traditionally awarded to Roman heroes as a sign of honor and respect.

ARSINOE IN CHAINS
Arsinoe was marched through the streets in chains as part of a huge parade to celebrate Caesar's victories in Gaul (France), Egypt, northwest Africa, and Turkey.

ANGRY CROWD
The Roman people thought it was wrong to treat Arsinoe this way and the guards had to use their spears to keep the angry crowd back.

CAESAR'S TRIUMPH

Caesar celebrated his victories by parading his captives through the streets of Rome. Cleopatra's sister, Arsinoe, who had led the Egyptian army against Caesar, was dragged through the streets bareheaded and in chains. It was a disgrace for a woman to appear in public this way – it was the custom for Roman women to wear a long cloak and veil outside their homes. However, Arsinoe was lucky; unlike other captives, she was not killed. Caesar feared that the Romans might riot if they saw a princess publicly executed.

> **I hate the queen ... although the gifts she promised me were of a literary nature and not beneath my dignity.**

Roman writer Cicero, after Cleopatra offered him books from the Alexandria library, from his *Letters to Atticus*, 44 BC

Temples and tributes

TO GIVE THANKS for his victory at the battle of Pharsalus, Julius Caesar built a new temple in Rome dedicated to Venus Genetrix (Venus the "Great Mother"). Caesar also paid for a beautiful statue of Cleopatra to be put on display in the temple – it showed her as a mother holding Caesarion in her arms.

A queen in Rome
Cleopatra stayed in one of Caesar's splendid villas in Rome. She held court there, inviting leading Romans to visit her and offering them rich gifts. She hoped to win their friendship and support.

Roman forum
This picture shows the ruins of the Roman forum (market square and meeting place) where Caesar built his temple to Venus Genetrix.

The goddess of love
Julius Caesar's family claimed descent from Venus. So it was a great honor for Cleopatra to have her statue in the temple.

THE DEATH OF CAESAR

As a reward for his victories, the Senate made Caesar dictator (sole ruler) for the next 10 years in 46 BC. Two years later, he was made dictator for life. But some Romans feared that Caesar was becoming too powerful, and that he wanted to be king. About sixty conspirators decided he must be killed.

The plot to murder Caesar was led by Brutus and Cassius.

Julius Caesar was stabbed to death after a Senate meeting in 44 BC.

Antony chose Quintus Dellius, who was known for his charm, to talk to Cleopatra on his behalf.

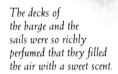

" Cleopatra sailed up the river Cydnus in a barge with a gilded poop, its sails spread purple, its rowers urging it on with silver oars to the sound of the flute blended with pipes and lute. "

Plutarch, from his
Life of Mark Antony,
c. AD 75

The sails were made of silk – a rare and costly cloth from China. Purple dye was so rare it was more expensive than gold.

AN URGENT SUMMONS

Antony had control of Egypt, but he needed Cleopatra's support, and he feared that she might side with his enemies. Antony needed Egypt's gold to pay his armies to keep control of his share of the empire, and Egypt's grain to feed his men. Antony wrote to Cleopatra and when she did not reply, he summoned her to meet him.

NO HURRY TO REPLY

Cleopatra was in no hurry to respond to Antony. Instead, she deliberately took her time. She knew that Antony needed Egypt's gold, and in return she planned to ask for his protection. She also wanted his help to kill her enemies – including her sister Arsinoe.

The decks of the barge and the sails were so richly perfumed that they filled the air with a sweet scent.

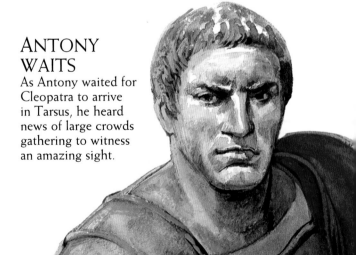

ANTONY WAITS

As Antony waited for Cleopatra to arrive in Tarsus, he heard news of large crowds gathering to witness an amazing sight.

ARRIVING IN STYLE

CAESAR'S MURDER LED TO THREE terrible years of civil war in Rome, as different groups of Roman senators and members of leading Roman families struggled to take control. The rival armies were led by three powerful men, and each hoped to take Caesar's place as ruler. Their names were Octavian (Caesar's nephew), Marcus Antonius (Antony), and Marcus Lepidus. Finally, in 42 BC the Roman lands were divided among them. Antony took control of the whole eastern Mediterranean region, which included Egypt.

Romans fighting Romans
Octavian, Antony, and Lepidus each had their own large armies of loyal, well-trained soldiers. They all fought against each other in a series of bitter battles. Leaders of the plot to kill Caesar also fought in this struggle for the right to rule Rome.

Antony was much older than Octavian. He was a tough, ruthless soldier, and he had won many great victories for Rome.

Lepidus was later forced to resign as joint ruler, after his soldiers deserted him and joined Octavian.

Octavian was young and inexperienced, but he was clever and very ambitious.

THREE RULERS FOR ROME

In order to win the struggle for power, Octavian, Antony, and Lepidus agreed to fight together against the armies led by Brutus and Cassius (the leaders in the plot to murder Caesar). In 42 BC, Antony's army defeated Brutus and Cassius at the Battle of Philippi. Octavian, Antony, and Lepidus then drew up a peace treaty, agreeing to rule Rome jointly for five years. Because Antony had won a great victory at Philippi, he was able to claim a greater share of the Roman empire, and the right to control Egypt was a rich prize.

TROUBLES AT HOME

AFTER CAESAR WAS MURDERED IN 44 BC, the shocking news spread like wildfire around the Roman world. Cleopatra – who was in Rome when the murder happened – lost no time in hurrying back to Egypt. Now that Caesar her protector was dead, her kingdom was once more in danger. Many hostile countries saw Egypt as a rich prize and hoped to conquer it. Cleopatra kept her son Caesarion close by her side, because she feared that he might be murdered by Caesar's enemies. Ptolemy XIV disappeared mysteriously, and people said that Cleopatra had poisoned her brother, so that she could rule Egypt with her young son.

Power struggle
Life back in Egypt was not easy for Cleopatra. She tried to win support from Alexandrian nobles by offering them rich rewards. She appeared in a "window of audience" in the royal palace and threw gifts to the crowd. But many people still saw her as a traitor, because of her friendship with Caesar and her long visit to Rome.

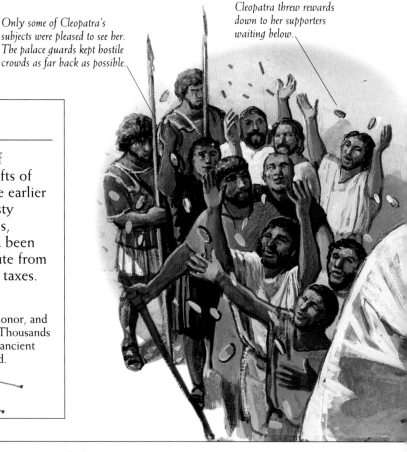

Only some of Cleopatra's subjects were pleased to see her. The palace guards kept hostile crowds as far back as possible.

Cleopatra threw rewards down to her supporters waiting below.

Rich rewards

TRADITIONALLY, PHAROAHS AND queens of Egypt rewarded loyal service with rich gifts of necklaces made from gold. Like earlier royal rulers, the Ptolemy dynasty had a huge store of gold, jewels, and other treasures, which had been given to past pharoahs as tribute from conquered peoples, or paid as taxes.

Collar of honor
This necklace is called a collar of honor, and is made from rows of gold rings. Thousands of years ago it was given to an ancient Egyptian noble as a reward.

FAMINE AND DISEASE

For two years during Cleopatra's reign, the Nile floods failed. There was not enough water in the river to spread rich mud over the fields or to irrigate them. As a result, farmers' crops and animals died, and many ordinary families suffered from famine and disease.

The steps and the marks on the walls helped to measure the water levels.

Flood forecast

The Nile floodwaters were very important to the Egyptian's survival so they measured the levels carefully every year. They built measuring devices, called Nilometers, along the banks of the river, so that they could check how fast the floodwaters were rising or draining away. When the floods failed, the fields baked hard in the hot sun and no crops could grow.

Women walked long distances in search of water for their families to drink.

Farm animals became thin and sickly through hunger, and many died.

Food was so scarce that families travelled great distances to go to market only to find there was nothing to buy there.

TROUBLEMAKERS!

On her return to Egypt, Cleopatra found out that her sister Arsinoe was plotting with Caesar's enemies and hoped to seize control of Egypt with their help. Many nobles in Cleopatra's court supported Arsinoe and joined in her conspiracy against Cleopatra.

Cleopatra is shown as a beautiful queen.

Caesarion is a powerful king.

ANGRY NOBLES

Many nobles and officials were angry that Cleopatra did not help the famine victims. But in fact, as Egypt produced most of the grain in the Roman world, there was nowhere else to buy supplies from.

Cleopatra and Caesarion

Cleopatra's son Caesarion was a toddler when she brought him back to Egypt. But Cleopatra paid for this carving to be made of them together. She wanted to remind all Egypt of their royal power.

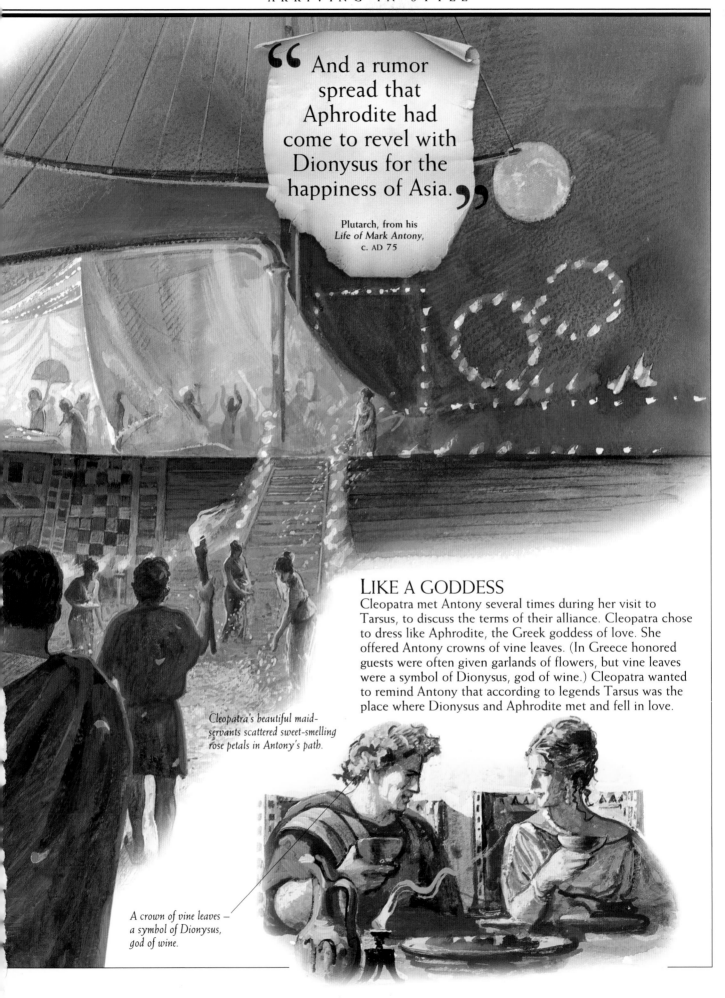

"And a rumor spread that Aphrodite had come to revel with Dionysus for the happiness of Asia."

Plutarch, from his
Life of Mark Antony,
c. AD 75

LIKE A GODDESS

Cleopatra met Antony several times during her visit to Tarsus, to discuss the terms of their alliance. Cleopatra chose to dress like Aphrodite, the Greek goddess of love. She offered Antony crowns of vine leaves. (In Greece honored guests were often given garlands of flowers, but vine leaves were a symbol of Dionysus, god of wine.) Cleopatra wanted to remind Antony that according to legends Tarsus was the place where Dionysus and Aphrodite met and fell in love.

Cleopatra's beautiful maid-servants scattered sweet-smelling rose petals in Antony's path.

A crown of vine leaves – a symbol of Dionysus, god of wine.

Mystery and Majesty

Antony had summoned Cleopatra to meet him in Tarsus (in Turkey), where he was getting ready to fight the warlike Parthians who lived to the east of Roman lands. Cleopatra knew that this meeting would decide Egypt's future. She had heard that Antony was a tough soldier, who loved pretty women and exotic luxuries. So Cleopatra planned a dramatic arrival, in a richly decorated boat, to impress him with her mystery, majesty, and charm.

FLOATING PALACE
Cleopatra's royal barge was built of the finest wood, with a gilded poop (a raised deck covered with gold).

ARRIVING IN TARSUS

The story of Cleopatra's arrival in Tarsus has inspired artists throughout history. This painting by Claude Lorrain shows Cleopatra being greeted by Antony. The buildings and ships are shown as they would have looked in the 17th century, not as they would have been in Cleopatra's time.

APHRODITE
Cleopatra was dressed as the goddess Aphrodite, and she lay on a couch beneath a canopy of gold cloth.

Music and dance

NO EGYPTIAN OR GREEK celebration was complete without music. Harps and lutes were favorites for banquets and parties, but palace musicians also played lyres, oboes, and tambourines. Cleopatra and her guests would have been entertained by singers, jesters, dancers, and acrobats.

Lyres were used to accompany singers or played by poets reciting their own verses.

Lutes could play fast, dramatic dance music, or soft, gentle love songs.

The air would have been filled with the sounds of music and clouds of rich perfume.

MAGICAL LIGHTS

After Cleopatra's spectacular arrival in Tarsus, Antony invited her to dine with him. But Cleopatra refused. Instead she insisted that he come to her royal barge. She took great care with her preparations – she wanted Antony to be delighted astonished, and most importantly, impressed. She arranged for her barge to be decorated with thousands of tiny oil lamps in glittering, flickering patterns of light.

ANTONY AND CLEOPATRA

CLEOPATRA'S DARING PLAN WORKED. Her dramatic visit to Tarsus had won Antony's support in her struggle to remain ruler of Egypt. Antony forgot his war against the Parthians and hurried to Egypt. Antony and Cleopatra spent the winter of 41 BC together in Alexandria, and Cleopatra hardly left Antony's side. She watched Antony exercise with his troops and took him on splendid boat trips down the Nile. She flattered him, listened to his battle stories, and entertained him at fabulous feasts. Cleopatra also became pregnant – with twins. Antony was their father, but he did not see them born. Early in 40 BC, Antony had to return to Rome because his wife, Fulvia, was leading a rebellion against Octavian.

Fragrant woods and perfum oils were burned, so that the air was filled with a sweet scent.

EXPENSIVE DELICACIES
Cleopatra ordered rare delicacies from all over the known world to be served at her feasts because she wanted to please and impress Antony.

Antony was proud of his strong, muscular physique. He liked to dress like the legendary Greek hero, Hercules, or the Greek god, Dionysus – the god of wine, song, and laughter.

At home in her royal palace, Cleopatra wore elegant Greek robes and delicate jewelry.

FABULOUS FEASTS

Cleopatra arranged lavish banquets to entertain Antony. Greek and Roman writers told how Cleopatra ordered twelve boars to be cooked, one after the other, so that one of them would be ready at the time Antony chose to eat. They also claimed that Antony and Cleopatra dressed up as servants and then went out into the streets of Alexandria after dark, playing tricks on people.

Guests lounged on couches, in typical Greek and Roman style. They would lean on their left arm and eat with their right hand.

DRINKING AND DANCING
The city of Alexandria was a sophisticated and luxurious city. And evenings spent drinking wine and dancing had always been popular in the palaces of the Ptolemies.

Musicians, acrobats, and dancers entertained guests at Cleopatra's feasts.

Like all the other Ptolemies, Cleopatra spared no expense to provide amusements and entertainments for her guests.

Guests lounged on their couches, eating from plates of food carried in by an army of servants.

Tables were set with gold and jeweled cups and plates. The couches were covered in the finest fabrics, often woven with gold and silver threads.

Extravagant stories
Stories abound about Cleopatra's extravagance. This 18th century painting was inspired by the story that Cleopatra dissolved a priceless pearl in wine and drank it. In fact, pearls are not harmed by wine.

Drinking cup
Alexandria was famous for producing beautifully decorated glassware, such as this pretty drinking cup.

Roman wedding
This carving shows a Roman wedding ceremony. Late in 40 BC, Antony's wife Fulvia died. Antony made a peace treaty with Octavian, and as a sign of friendship he married Octavian's sister, Octavia.

QUEEN OF KINGS

CLEOPATRA CONTINUED TO RULE EGYPT, but Antony did not return for nearly four years. When he sailed back in 36 BC after a disastrous defeat in Parthia, Cleopatra welcomed him. She needed a strong ally to help her keep Egypt independent. Antony was bold and ambitious, and he had huge armies of loyal soldiers who were ready to fight for him. Antony planned to set up an empire in north Africa and the Middle East to challenge his rivals in Rome, and Cleopatra supported his plans because they would increase her own power. In 35 BC Cleopatra and Antony had a third child, a son who they named Ptolemy Philadelphus. Early in 34 BC, Antony invaded Armenia and returned to Alexandria in triumph, and in a magnificent ceremony Cleopatra was crowned "Queen of Kings," and all her children were given special royal titles.

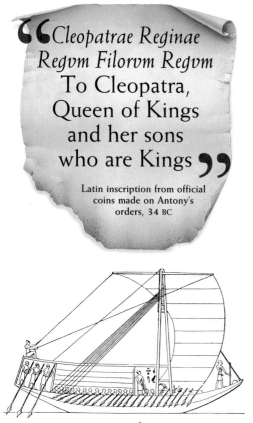

A fleet of warships
Cleopatra needed warships to defend Egypt and keep control of the Middle Eastern lands that she and Antony claimed as part of their empire. Skilled Egyptian shipbuilders used timber from Middle Eastern lands, especially Syria, to construct a mighty fleet.

ROYAL TITLES
Cleopatra and Antony gave royal titles to their young children – they were named as rulers of the Middle Eastern lands that Antony controlled. It was a sign of their alliance and ambition.

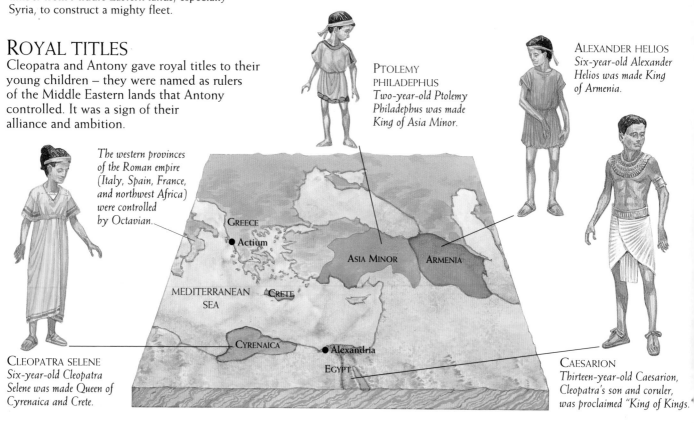

The western provinces of the Roman empire (Italy, Spain, France, and northwest Africa) were controlled by Octavian.

PTOLEMY PHILADEPHUS
Two-year-old Ptolemy Philadephus was made King of Asia Minor.

ALEXANDER HELIOS
Six-year-old Alexander Helios was made King of Armenia.

CLEOPATRA SELENE
Six-year-old Cleopatra Selene was made Queen of Cyrenaica and Crete.

CAESARION
Thirteen-year-old Caesarion, Cleopatra's son and coruler, was proclaimed "King of Kings."

ROYAL CROWN
As Queen of Kings, Cleopatra wore a crown with three snakes' heads. To the ancient Egyptians, the cobra was a sign of royal power.

PRECIOUS PEARLS
Pearls from the Indian Ocean were rare and valuable.

An ankh is an Egyptian symbol of life.

A cornucopia (horn of plenty), a Greek symbol of prosperity.

GREAT AMBITIONS

With Antony to help her, Cleopatra hoped to make Egypt the rich, civilized, and successful empire it had been when the first Ptolemies ruled, almost 300 years before. Cleopatra planned to reclaim the lands that the Ptolemies had once controlled outside Egypt. Many of these, including Syria, Lebanon, Phoenicia, and parts of Asia Minor, were given to her by Antony.

Royal reminder
In 34 BC Antony had silver coins made which showed Cleopatra's portrait and the inscription "Queen of Kings" on one side, and Antony's portrait on the other. It was a reminder of Cleopatra's royal power and a sign of their joint ambition.

Traitor!
When Octavian heard about Antony and Cleopatra's ambitious plans, he made powerful speeches in the Roman senate, declaring Antony as a traitor who no longer deserved the support of any Roman senator, citizen, or soldier.

A Roman senator

War with Rome

TOP ROMAN POLITICIANS, LED BY CAESAR'S nephew Octavian, were shocked by reports of Antony and Cleopatra's bid to set up an empire of their own. They were also angry that Antony had divorced his Roman wife. Late in 32 BC Octavian led a procession to Rome's temple of Bellona, goddess of war. Hurling a blood-tipped spear through the air, he declared war against Cleopatra – and all Egypt. Octavian knew that Antony still had supporters in Rome. But he felt sure the Romans would unite to fight against Egypt's ambitious queen.

This painting of the Battle of Actium (in the style of Eugen Schoen) is from *Panorama of World History*, by M. Reymond.

Battle-ax

Dagger

Short sword

A variety of weapons were used at this time. While Egyptian soldiers fought with battle-axes and hatchets, Roman soldiers used three main weapons — a long sword, for slashing; a short sword, for stabbing, and a dagger, for close combat.

" Antony bore witness to Caesarion that he was sprung from Caesar... gave enormous presents to his children by the Egyptian queen... and ordered that his body be buried by her side. "

Dio Cassius, from his *Roman History*, c. AD 155

THE BATTLE OF ACTIUM

As Cleopatra's friend and Octavian's rival, Antony joined in the war against Rome. Antony also did not want to lose control of his lands in the east of the Roman empire, which included Greece. Fearing an attack by Rome, Antony and Cleopatra sailed to Greece with a huge fleet of warships. In spring 31 BC the Roman forces arrived, and for several months Octavian's fleet patrolled the Greek coast, fighting Antony's soldiers, capturing his forts and sinking his ships. Worst of all, they trapped Antony and Cleopatra's fleet in the Gulf of Ambracia. The land around the gulf was marshy and damp, and in the summer heat the soldiers and sailors became very ill with malaria, food and water supplies ran out, and many of them deserted. By September, the situation was desperate. Antony and Cleopatra decided that they must try to smash through the Roman blockade.

Helping hands
Antony and Cleopatra's army was made up of Roman and Egyptian soldiers, together with soldiers from many different lands. The kings of countries controlled by Antony, such as Libya, Cilicia (part of modern Turkey), and Arabia, sent soldiers to fight with Antony.

ADMIRAL AGRIPPA
Octavian's advisers included Marcus Vispanius Agrippa (64 BC–12 BC) one of Rome's most famous army commanders. Octavian knew that he could trust Agrippa, and that he understood naval strategy and tactics far better than Antony or Cleopatra.

Agrippa

Octavian

Octavian's camp

SAILS READY!
Egyptian and Roman warships did not usually carry sails into battle, because they were heavy and took up valuable space. Instead, warships were powered by men rowing with oars. Before the Battle of Actium Antony and Cleopatra ordered their warships to have sails ready to hoist. They hoped to smash through the Roman blockade, and sail away as soon as they reached the open sea.

BATTLE TACTICS

Both sides made careful plans before fighting the Battle of Actium in September 31 BC. Octavian aimed to lure Antony and Cleopatra's ships out of the gulf, and then overpower them with his much larger fleet. Antony gave orders for his ships to fight their way through the middle of the Roman blockade.

FACT file

- When Antony and Cleopatra arrived in Greece at the beginning of the campaign they had about 300 Roman and 200 Egyptian warships. By the Battle of Actium they only had about 230 ships, and about 20,000 soldiers.

- Octavian had about 400 ships in his fleet and 37,000 soldiers.

- Cleopatra managed to escape with her own squadron of 60 ships, which included her treasure ship.

Gulf of Ambracia

• **Actium**

TRAPPED! Cleopatra and Antony's warships were moored inside the Gulf of Ambracia, near Actium. The only way out of the gulf was to sail out into the Ionian sea.

• **Antony's camp**

IONIAN SEA

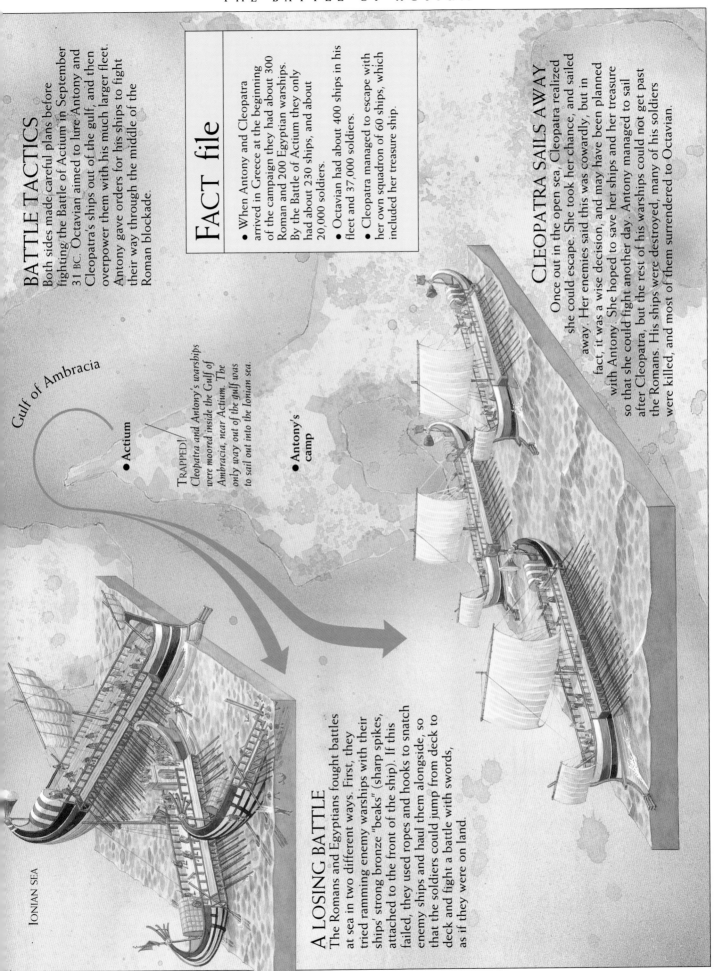

A LOSING BATTLE

The Romans and Egyptians fought battles at sea in two different ways. First, they tried ramming enemy warships with their ships' strong bronze "beaks" (sharp spikes) attached to the front of the ship). If this failed, they used ropes and hooks to snatch enemy ships and haul them alongside, so that the soldiers could jump from deck to deck and fight a battle with swords, as if they were on land.

CLEOPATRA SAILS AWAY

Once out in the open sea, Cleopatra realized she could escape. She took her chance, and sailed away. Her enemies said this was cowardly, but in fact, it was a wise decision, and may have been planned with Antony. She hoped to save her ships and her treasure so that she could fight another day. Antony managed to sail after Cleopatra, but the rest of his warships could not get past the Romans. His ships were destroyed, many of his soldiers were killed, and most of them surrendered to Octavian.

Victorious return
After the Battle of Actium, Cleopatra sailed back into Alexandria harbor with flags flying as if she had won a great victory. She was afraid her enemies might not let her back into the city if they knew that she had been defeated by Octavian.

To the shores of the Red Sea
To protect her fleet from the Romans, Cleopatra ordered that her warships be hauled overland, from the Meditteranean to the Red Sea. But one of Cleopatra's neighbors and enemies, the King of Nabatea, set fire to the warships and destroyed them all.

STONE CARVING
Skilled stoneworkers would have worked on Cleopatra's tomb. They decorated the outside with beautiful designs, carved into the surface of the stone.

MAGNIFICENT MAUSOLEUM
Cleopatra knew that her future was uncertain if Octavian invaded Egypt. She began to experiment with poisons, and gave orders that work on her mausoleum (large tomb chamber) be completed as soon as possible.

DEFEAT AND DISHONOR

DEFEAT AT THE BATTLE OF ACTIUM plunged Antony into despair. He hid away on Pharos, an island in Alexandria harbor, and refused to see anyone. But Cleopatra bravely made plans to continue as Egypt's ruler. Her spies told her that Octavian did not have enough gold to pay his armies, so he could not attack immediately. But Cleopatra knew Octavian would attack sooner or later, because he needed Egypt's wealth. In time, Antony came out of hiding, and once again splendid banquets were held in the palace. Almost a year after Actium, the news came – the Romans were on their way. Cleopatra sent a message to Octavian, offering to give up her throne if he would let her children rule. But Octavian did not reply – and it was clear that Octavian wanted to rule Egypt himself, for Rome. Antony rallied his army and rode out of the city to face Octavian.

GOLD AND JEWELS

As soon as her mausoleum was completed, Cleopatra gave orders for her treasures to be stored there. She believed that her spirit would survive after death to enjoy them. More importantly, she wanted to keep her gold and jewels safe. Cleopatra announced that she would set fire to the mausoleum and destroy the treasure if the Roman army marched on Alexandria.

Hellenistic (Greek) gold earrings

EGYPT'S WEALTH

Octavian invaded Egypt because he needed gold. It is reported that he had all of Cleopatra's treasure melted down, so that he could make coins to pay his armies.

ROYAL TOMB

Cleopatra's mausoleum was probably built in the Ptolemies' royal cemetery, near the tomb of Alexander the Great. Its remains are yet to be found.

Precious stones and metals such as turquoise and gold were mined in Egypt to make beautiful jewelry.

A gold falcon, symbol of the Egyptian god Horus

Beautiful tombs were important to Greeks and Egyptians. They were houses in which they believed the dead person's spirit lived.

> **All swore to end their lives together, and until that time they charmed their days with a succession of glorious banquets.**
>
> Plutarch, from his
> *Life of Mark Antony*
> c. AD 75

Dionysus holds a bunch of grapes, symbol of wine.

Dionysus, god of wine, song, and laughter

DIONYSUS

Antony believed that he was protected by the god Dionysus. Sometimes he felt he had become the god. The Greek historian Plutarch tells a chilling story: the night before Octavian marched on Alexandria, the citizens heard the sound of laughter and footsteps leaving the city. They said this showed that Dionysus had deserted Antony.

The death of Antony

ANTONY WAS FORCED to flee from Octavian's army when most of his soldiers refused to fight. Antony was disgraced and ashamed, and he blamed Cleopatra. Afraid of his anger, Cleopatra locked herself in her mausoleum and sent a message saying she was dead. In despair, Antony stabbed himself. When she heard this Cleopatra sent her servants to carry Antony to her, and he died in her arms.

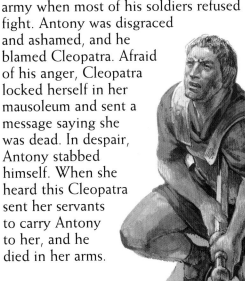

THE DEATH OF CLEOPATRA

WITHIN WEEKS OF ANTONY'S SUICIDE in 30 BC, Cleopatra was dead, and Egypt was governed by Rome. Cleopatra was the last independent ruler of Egypt, and her death marked the end of over 3,000 glorious years of Egyptian civilization and Egyptian power. Although she did her best to defend her country, clever, charming Cleopatra could not defy the might of Rome. After Antony died, Roman troops surrounded Cleopatra's mausoleum, and kept her prisoner there. But Octavian treated her well. He allowed Cleopatra to arrange Antony's funeral, and to take part in the ceremony. But, he would not agree to let Cleopatra's children rule Egypt on behalf of Rome. So Cleopatra decided she must die. She could not bear to live while foreigners ruled her land. At her death, Egypt lost its most famous – and possibly its greatest – queen.

Carvings and columns
This funeral stele (carved upright stone) gives an idea of the style of buildings in the time of the Ptolemies. The doorway to Cleopatra's mausoleum may have looked like this.

" Then somebody said in anger: "A fine deed, this, Charmion!" "It is indeed most fine," she said, "and befitting the descendant of so many kings." **"**

Plutarch, from his
Life of Mark Antony
c. AD 75

A FINAL FEAST

It is said that before her death Cleopatra ordered a splendid feast. She then asked one of her servants to smuggle in a poisonous snake in a basket of figs. After Cleopatra had eaten, she sent a note to Octavian asking to be buried with Antony. Alarmed, Octavian sent guards to find her, but it was too late. Cleopatra was already dead.

Guardian goddesses
This painting on a sarcophagus (stone coffin) shows the goddess Isis and her sister Nephthys watching over a dead body. In Egyptian legends they brought the dead back to life.

A mysterious end

CLEOPATRA'S BODY HAS never been discovered, so historians do not know exactly how she died. There are stories that she experimented with poisons, and that she even tested some of them on slaves.

Bitten by an asp
The most popular story about Cleopatra's death says that she was bitten by a small poisonous snake, called an asp. But an asp would not have been able to bite Cleopatra and her two servants.

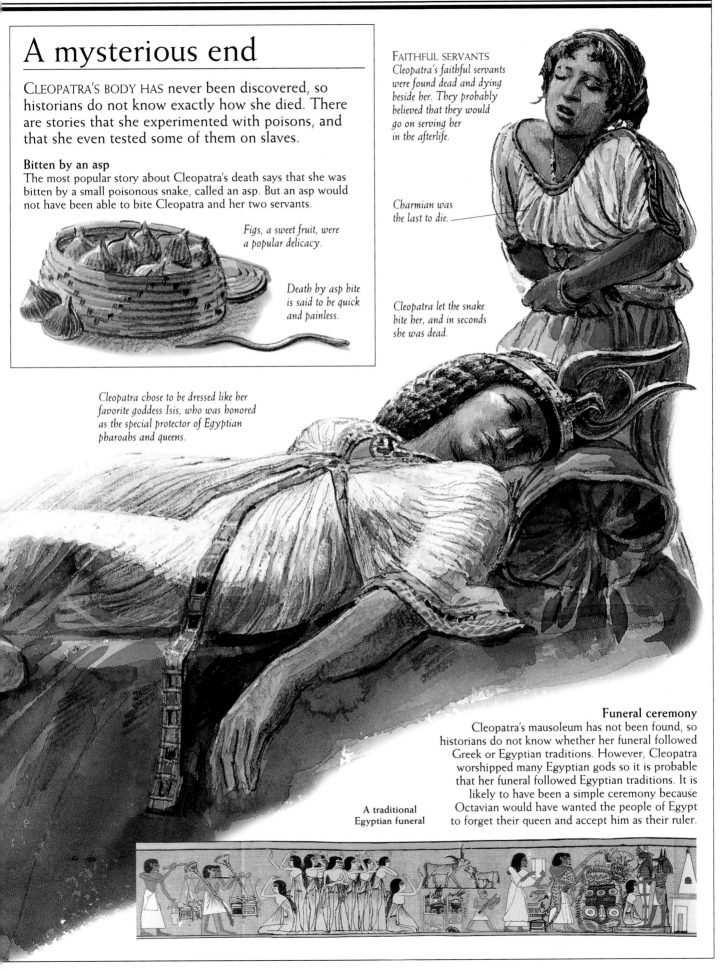

Figs, a sweet fruit, were a popular delicacy.

Death by asp bite is said to be quick and painless.

FAITHFUL SERVANTS
Cleopatra's faithful servants were found dead and dying beside her. They probably believed that they would go on serving her in the afterlife.

Charmian was the last to die.

Cleopatra let the snake bite her, and in seconds she was dead.

Cleopatra chose to be dressed like her favorite goddess Isis, who was honored as the special protector of Egyptian pharoahs and queens.

Funeral ceremony
Cleopatra's mausoleum has not been found, so historians do not know whether her funeral followed Greek or Egyptian traditions. However, Cleopatra worshipped many Egyptian gods so it is probable that her funeral followed Egyptian traditions. It is likely to have been a simple ceremony because Octavian would have wanted the people of Egypt to forget their queen and accept him as their ruler.

A traditional Egyptian funeral

43

AFTER CLEOPATRA

The death of Cleopatra made it easy for Octavian and the Roman army to complete their conquest of Egypt. In 30 bc, Octavian declared himself to be the new pharoah of Egypt. To show that they were now in control, Roman soldiers defaced ancient Egyptian monuments and destroyed official documents – including most of those created while Cleopatra was in power. For the next 500 years, Egypt became part of the Roman empire, ruled by governors appointed by Rome. Alexandria continued to be a great center of learning and trade, but elsewhere Egypt's power and prosperity began to decline.

The Nile crocodile was an instantly recognizable symbol of Egypt.

Egypt captured
In 28 BC Roman leader Octavian issued this coin – the Latin words mean "Egypt captured" – to commemorate the death of Cleopatra and Antony and to celebrate Rome's conquest of Egypt.

This stone head probably represents Cleopatra's eldest son Caesarion. He tried to flee to Syria but was betrayed by his tutor. Octavian had Caesarion executed.

CLEOPATRA'S CHILDREN

Historians think that Cleopatra's younger children – Cleopatra Selene, Alexander Helios, and Ptolemy Philadelphus – were sent to live with Antony's wife Octavia in Rome. The boys were never heard of again. But Cleopatra Selene married King Juba of Mauretania (a country in north Africa), and she called one of her sons Ptolemy.

HOMAGE TO A HERO

After Octavian had completed his conquest of Egypt, he went to visit the tomb of Alexander the Great in Alexandria. Cleopatra VII – and the Ptolemy dynasty (family) – were descended from one of Alexander the Great's generals. When Octavian was asked if he wanted to visit the tombs of the Ptolemies, he said he had come to honor a hero, not to see dead kings and queens.

ALEXANDER THE GREAT (356–323 BC)

Cleopatra's place in history
Cleopatra's death marked the end of an era in Egyptian history.

THE PYRAMIDS AT GIZA WERE BUILT C. 2,500 BC

343–332 BC PERSIAN KINGS RULED EGYPT

323–30 BC THE PTOLEMIES RULED EGYPT

51–30 BC CLEOPATRA VII (69–30 BC) RULED EGYPT

| 500 BC | 400 BC | 300 BC | 200 BC | 100 BC | 0 |

C. 3,100–343 BC EGYPTIAN PHAROAHS RULED EGYPT

332 BC ALEXANDER THE GREAT CONQUERED EGYPT

31 BC BATTLE OF ACTIUM

OCTAVIAN IN TRIUMPH

A year after Cleopatra died, Octavian staged a huge triumph (victory procession) to celebrate his conquest of Egypt. Antony and Cleopatra's children were probably made to march in the procession, alongside Cleopatra's fabulous treasures.

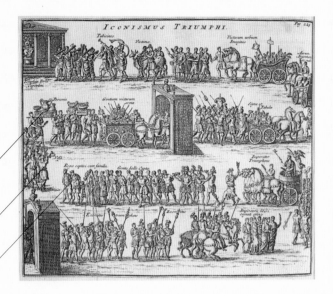

Gold and silver treasures were held high for all to see.

Weapons, armor, and other trophies were put on display.

Defeated rulers and their families were marched along in chains.

Laurel leaves
It was traditional for victorious Roman generals to be crowned with a laurel wreath.

Roman Egypt

AFTER EGYPT WAS conquered by Rome, it was known as the "Granary (grain store) of the Roman empire." The empire needed huge amounts of wheat to feed Rome's vast army and the people who lived in the fast-growing cities, especially Rome. Other Egyptian products were popular in Rome, such as fine linens, papyrus, and perfumed oils. Egyptian scholars, poets, scientists, and gladiators were famous throughout the Roman world.

WHEAT

Fine papers
Papyrus (paper made from reeds grown in the Nile Delta) was exported to the lands of the Roman empire.

The Julian Calendar

In 46 BC, Roman leader Julius Caesar made changes to the Roman calendar, using scientific ideas first discovered by Greek and Egyptian astronomers, working together in Cleopatra's capital, Alexandria. Under the rule of the Ptolemies, the city became a great center of learning, and visitors like Caesar carried Egyptian ideas and discoveries back to Rome. The calendar that is used in most countries today is based on these ideas.

This pocket sundial uses shadows cast by the string pointer to measure time. The astronomers of Ancient Egypt were the first to use the movements of the sun to measure time.

MARK ANTONY

FORGOTTEN HERO?

Most of Mark Antony's statues were destroyed on Octavian's orders, but a wealthy Alexandrian paid to save Cleopatra's statues. Antony may have been forgotten in Egypt, but his image has survived on many Roman coins, and he was grandfather and great-grandfather to three Roman emperors – Caligula, Claudius, and Nero.

AD 43 ROMANS INVADE AND CONQUER BRITAIN

AD 324 ROMAN EMPEROR CONSTANTINE DECLARES CHRISTIANITY THE OFFICIAL RELIGION OF THE ROMAN EMPIRE, INCLUDING EYGPT

C. 600–900 AD MUSLIM SOLDIERS AND SETTLERS FROM THE MIDDLE EAST BRING ISLAM TO EGYPT

AD 100	AD 200	AD 300	AD 400	AD 500	AD 600

27 BC–AD 14 OCTAVIAN (CAESAR AUGUSTUS) EMPEROR OF ROME

AD 395 ROMAN EMPIRE DIVIDED, WITH WESTERN EMPIRE BASED IN ROME AND EASTERN EMPIRE BASED IN CONSTANTINOPLE, TURKEY

AD 476 WESTERN ROMAN EMPIRE COMES TO AN END

CLEOPATRA'S STORY —
FACT AND FICTION

Coins are often the only visual evidence that has survived.

Cleopatra VII is one of the most famous women who ever lived. Her story has inspired poets, dramatists, and artists for over 2,000 years, and still fascinates us today. But, in fact, we know very little about her. The details of her life have been lost, or are shrouded in mystery. Only fragments of official documents dating from her reign have survived to tell us about her thoughts and deeds, and only a few carvings and sculptures remain to show us what she looked like. Most of our knowledge of Cleopatra comes from Greek and Roman writers who were loyal to Rome and did not approve of her.

Hieroglyphs
Cleopatra's name would have been carved or written, using Egyptian hieroglyphs (pictures and symbols), on temple walls and royal decrees.

Queen Cleopatra
Some Ptolemaic queens, including Cleopatra VII, issued coins bearing their portraits. The coins are beautiful and were probably designed to create a good public image. This gold coin bears the portrait of another Ptolemaic queen – Cleopatra I.

A Greek name
Greek was the official language of Egypt in Cleopatra's time. So her name would also have been carved or written in Greek letters, as here.

Portrait of a queen
We can tell that this carving represents a Ptolemaic queen because it shows a royal crown and an elaborate Greek hairstyle of corkscrew curls. It is a portrait of Cleopatra I or II.

WHICH CLEOPATRA?
Some sculptures inscribed (carved) with the name "Cleopatra" have survived. But there were at least seven queens named Cleopatra in the Ptolemaic dynasty (ruling family), and Cleopatra VII was the last.

ALEXANDRIA UNDER THE SEA
Alexandria is a big, modern city today, but the royal quarter where Cleopatra VII lived was flooded after an earthquake in the 14th century AD. In 1992, French archeologist Franck Goddio and a team of divers started to explore the site. They have found a variety of statues and artefacts, and hope to find the lost palace of Cleopatra.

From hearsay to history

THE GREEK HISTORIAN, Plutarch (c. AD 50–120) described Cleopatra in his biography (life story) of Mark Antony. Plutarch started to write his stories almost a hundred years after Cleopatra lived. He based his work on eyewitness accounts collected by his grandfather Lamprias, and on documents which no longer survive today. It is difficult to tell whether his stories about Cleopatra are true.

PLUTARCH

Parallel lives
His *Life of Mark Antony* is one of a series of texts in which Plutarch compared Greek and Roman heroes.

WILLIAM SHAKESPEARE

ANTONY AND CLEOPATRA
Over 1,500 years after Plutarch died, English playwright William Shakespeare (1554–1616) was inspired by Plutarch's stories to write a play about Cleopatra and her love for Antony.

BEAUTIFUL FANTASY
Writers, artists, and later, filmmakers have been inspired by Cleopatra throughout history. Artist Sir Lawrence Alma-Tadema (1836–1912) painted imaginary scenes from Ancient Egypt and Rome. Here, he imagines Cleopatra as she waited for Antony in Tarsus.

CARRY ON CLEO
The legend of Cleopatra has inspired comedy as well as tragedy. The 1965 comic film *Carry on Cleo* portrayed Cleopatra as pretty and quite powerful, but not really suitable to be queen. Throughout history, people have often refused to take women rulers seriously.

PLAY FOR TODAY
William Shakespeare's play, *Antony and Cleopatra*, brilliantly brought the tragic love story of Cleopatra and Antony to life. Portraying a strong character like Cleopatra is a challenge relished by many actresses. In this scene from the play, staged in London, England in 1999, the role of Cleopatra is played by British star Helen Mirren.

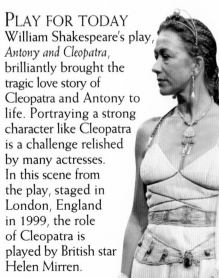

HOLLYWOOD BLOCKBUSTER
In 1963, Hollywood filmmakers completed a screen epic about Cleopatra and Antony. It starred a real-life couple, Elizabeth Taylor and Richard Burton, but it was not historically accurate. This scene from the film shows a lavish feast.

Index

Acknowledgments

The publisher would like to thank: Rachel Hilford, Sally Hamilton and Diane Legrande for picture research; Selina Wood for editorial help; David Gillingwater for early visuals; and Chris Bernstein for the index.

The publisher would like to thank the following for their kind permission to reproduce their photographs:

a=above; b=below; c=center; l=left; r=right; t=top

AKG London: 19tr, 36-37; Cameraphoto, State Art Museum, Bucharest: *Cleopatra Dissolves the Pearl* Anton Schoonyans 33tr; Erich Lessing 40cl.
Ancient Art & Architecture Collection: 27br, 45cb, 46tr; Dr. S. Coyne 9tl; G. T. Garvey 17cr; Ronald Sheridan 2cl, 8tl, 33cr, 41tl.
Dr Sally-Ann Ashton: 15tr.
Bildarchiv Preußischer Kulturbesitz: Antikenmuseum: Johannes Laurentius 13.
Bridgeman Art Library, London/New York: Antony and Cleopatra Sir Lawrence Alma-

Tadema 47tr; Louvre, France: Cleopatra Disembarking at Tarsus Claude Lorrain 30tl.
British Museum, London: 19cr, 20cla, 20cl, 20t, 21tc, 25tr, 26bl, 33br, 35cra, 35crb, 37tl, 41cr, 45cbl.
Mary Evans Picture Library: 6-7, 25b, 43br, 47tl.
Werner Forman Archive: British Museum 44tr; Private Collection 21tr.
Ronald Grant Archive: Carry on Cleo 1963 © EMI/Peter Roger's Production 47cr; Cleopatra 1963 © Twentieth Century Fox 24tr, 47bl.
Performing Arts Library: Fritz

Curzon 47br.
Popperfoto: 46br.
Scala Group S.p.A.: Arte romana Vaticano Cortile delle Corazze 0tl; Vaticano Museo Gregoriano Egizio 41cla.
Science Museum: 14br, 45cr.

Jacket: **Ancient Art & Architecture Collection:** front cl.
Bildarchiv Preußischer Kulturbesitz, Berlin 2000: Antikenmuseum: Johannes Laurentius front cll.
Scala Group S.p.A.: Vaticano Museo Gregoriano Egizio back cr.